EASY ORGAN CLASSICS

Edited by
ROLLIN SMITH

DOVER PUBLICATIONS, INC.
Mineola, New York

MW00444829

Copyright

Copyright © 2006 by Dover Publications, Inc.
All rights reserved.

Bibliographical Note

This Dover edition, first published in 2006, is a new compilation of works from early authoritative editions. A number of titles have been newly engraved by Rollin Smith especially for this edition.

International Standard Book Number: 0-486-44957-2

Manufactured in the United States of America
Dover Publications, Inc., 31 East 2nd Street, Mineola, N.Y. 11501

EASY ORGAN MUSIC

NOTES ON THE MUSIC

JOHANN SEBASTIAN BACH
PASTORALE

Clearly influenced by the organ pastorales of Frescobaldi, Pasquini, and Zipoli, the *Pastorale* dates from Bach's Weimar Period (1708–1717). As in the Italian models, Bach's work derives from the custom of the shepherds who provided music for Christmas festivals in Rome.

JOHANNES BRAHMS
O WORLD, I E'EN MUST LEAVE THEE
Op. 22, No. 11

Brahms wrote his *Eleven Chorale Preludes* in May and June 1896, immediately after completing the *Four Serious Songs,* Op. 121; they mark the conclusion of his work as a creative artist. This, Brahms's last composition, is not expressive of grief but rather of trust and anticipation of the future life. The melody is a folksong by Heinrich Isaak (1450–1517) and appears in many hymnals as the tune INNSBRUCK. The anonymous 16th-century text begins:

> O world, I must leave thee; My Lord
> will soon receive me,
> For I am homeward bent.
> My body, life, and spirit, And ev'rything
> I merit
> I place in God's most gracious hand.

LAMBERT CHAUMONT
TRIO PAR CONTRAFUGUE
VOIX HUMAINE

Lambert Chaumont was born sometime between 1630 and 1635, studied in Liège, Belgium, and was later ordained a priest in Reims. In 1672 he was appointed pastor of the Church of Saint-Martin in Huy (a small village between Namur and Liège) and sixteen years later pastor of Saint-Germain in the same city. That Father Chaumont did not spend much time working on sermons is evident from his 111 short pieces in the eight ecclesiastical modes. Published in 1695, they were intended for use as interludes, or *versets,* in alternation with the choir. In the *Trio par Contrafugue* alternate entrances are in inversion while the *Voix Humaine* demonstrates the entire range of the reed stop intended to imitate the human voice.

LOUIS COUPERIN
CHACONE IN F MAJOR

Born in Chaumes about 1626, Louis Couperin went to Paris with his teacher, the clavecinist Jacques Chambonnières, around 1650, was organist of Saint-Gervais for a dozen years, and died at the early age of 35. Louis Couperin was the uncle of François Couperin (Le Grand) and the first of eight members of the family, who for 170 successive years occupied the organist post of Saint-Gervais.

The grandly expressive *Chaconne in F Minor,* composed in 1658, is typical of Louis Couperin's vigorous style with dark color, relentless power, and aggressive dissonances.

JEAN-FRANÇOIS DANDRIEU
OFFERTOIRE FOR EASTER

Dandrieu was appointed organist of the Church of Saint-Merry in January 1704 and was later a member of the French chapel royal. This Offertory for Easter Day is based on the melody with which the 15th-century Latin Easter hymn, "O Filii et Filiæ" (Ye Sons and Daughters) has always been associated.

ARTHUR FOOTE
CANTILÈNE

When he graduated from Harvard, Arthur Foote received the first M.A. degree in music to be granted by an American university. He was organist of the First Unitarian Church in Boston from 1878 to 1910 and was a founder, and at one time warden, of the American Guild of Organists.

Cantilène, one of a set of *Seven Pieces,* Op. 71, was published in 1912.

CÉSAR FRANCK
ANDANTINO IN G MINOR

Composed while César Franck was organist of Saint-Jean-Saint-François Church in the Marais, this *Andantino* was his first published organ work. It appeared in 1857 in the fourth volume of Georges Schmitt's *Musée de l'organiste.* It is in simple ABA form with a coda. It was probably played by the composer for the first time at Cavaillé-Coll's factory on August 30, 1856, when Franck demonstrated the organ built for the Cathedral of Carcassonne.

OFFERTOIRE IN G MINOR

This early work of Franck, completed on September 13, 1859, was not published during his lifetime. After Franck's death, his son collected a number of manuscripts and had them published by Enoch in 1905. When Charles Tournemire edited them in 1933 as the second volume of *L'Organiste,* he gave this Offertoire the title *Pièce symphonique.* As such it might be regarded as an early study for the *Grande Pièce symphonique* of 1863. Four different themes make up this work: a march, declamatory chords marked "très largement;" a chorale, and a sinuous line of triplets which, when heard together with the march, provide a brief development.

CHARLES GOUNOD
OFFERTORIUM
COMMUNION

After his two-and-one-half year stay at the Villa Medici in Rome when he won the Grand Prix de Rome in 1839, Gounod began his professional life in November 1843 as organist and maître-de-chapelle of the Église des Missions Étrangères in Paris. In 1877 he took the post of organist at the parish church in the western Parisian suburb of Saint-Cloud and played there for over ten years.

In all, the composer of *Faust* wrote about ten organ works. The *Communion* (in C) was printed in *La Maîtrise,* a Parisian music journal published by Au Ménestrel, just beginning its second year, with the April 15, 1858, issue.

In 1876, the Music & Art Association of London published the *Offertorium.* Because the pedal part descends to A below the low C of the organ's pedalboard, it is possible that the composer was thinking of the pédalier, or pedal piano.

GEORGE FRIDERIC HANDEL
PRELUDE AND FUGUE IN D MAJOR

The Prelude is in the style of a French Overture, written with dotted rhythms. Both the prelude and fugue are in three voices and can be played entirely on the manuals, but a few Pedal notes have been added for a more grandiose effect.

CONCERTO NO. 13 IN F MAJOR

There are few works in organ literature so splendidly vigorous as the organ concertos that Handel wrote for the 18th-century London public. They occupy a unique place not only for their unaffected secular nature but because they have no predecessors and (with few exceptions in England) no successors. The concertos date from the later period of Handel's life when his genius came to fruition in the great oratorios. He would play these concertos at oratorio performances, where his characteristic "grand manner" of playing in a "new organ concerto" often proved the chief attraction.

This concerto was completed on April 2, 1739; two nights later it was heard for the first time in a performance of *Israel in Egypt* at the King's Theatre, London. It has long been known as "The Cuckoo and the Nightingale" because of the endearing bird imitations in the second movement. He probably introduced the birdsong because it would be appropriate on an April evening.

In September and October of the same year Handel reworked the second and third movements as the Allegro and Larghetto of the Concerto Grosso in F, Op. 6, No. 9. The first and final movements are based on the first and second movements of the Trio Sonata, Op. 5, No. 6.

This keyboard arrangement is based on the 1740 London edition published by John Walsh. It was intended for private use by musical amateurs and is a two-part reduction of the orchestral and organ parts. In this first version, the Allegro is 119 measures long. When reworked as a Concerto grosso it was reduced to 109 measures, and when Handel altered the manuscript sometime after 1744/45, it was further abbreviated to 100 measures—the version of the organ concerto that we know today.

FRANZ JOSEPH HAYDN
ANDANTINO

During the 17th and 18th centuries, musical clocks were popular with the German nobility. The more important examples had a mechanical pipe organ built into a floor clock and was usually called a *Flötenuhren* or Flute Clock. Haydn wrote 31 charming works for flute clocks built by Primitivus Niemecz, a priest friend and pupil who was librarian to Prince Nicholas Esterhazy. This Andantino was composed in 1792 and bears the unmistakable mark of Haydn's gracious style.

JOSEPH JONGEN
CHORAL, Op. 37, No. 4

Joseph Jongen's entire musical training took place at the Liège Conservatory, where, in addition to many prizes, he won the Grand Prix de Rome in 1897. He was appointed professor of harmony and counterpoint in 1902.

From 1925 until his retirement in 1939 Jongen was director of the Brussels Conservatory.

Though impressionism makes itself felt in some of his finest works, Jongen is more indebted to Franck than to Debussy. The *Choral* from *Quatre Pièces,* Op. 37, was completed on January 17, 1911 and given its first performance by Léandre Vilain in Ostend on July 5 the same year. Joseph Bonnet, the eminent French virtuoso and organist of Saint-Eustache, considered it the work of a great musician and frequently performed it.

SIGFRID KARG-ELERT
IMPROVISATION ON "NEARER, MY GOD, TO THEE"

Karg-Elert, successor to Max Reger as professor of composition at the Leipzig Conservatory and one of the most prolific organ composers in the instrument's history (200 works), was the first to advance organ composition to the realm of impressionism. His mature style is introspective, harmonically rich, and marked by an almost kaleidoscopic efflorescence of tone colors. The composer has added the following program note for this Improvisation published in 1913:

On the 15th of April, 1912, the colossal English steamer *Titanic* collided with a floating iceberg in the Atlantic Ocean. Over 1,600 people met their death in this tragedy. As the ship sank, the passengers sang "Nearer, My God, To Thee."

JOHANN LUDWIG KREBS
O GOD! HEAR MY SIGHS

Krebs was a chorister under Bach and later one of his most talented pupils. He was so successful an imitator of his master that the authorship of some pieces existing in the autograph of each cannot be determined. He was regarded during his lifetime as an extraordinary organist. The hymn tune is set to a text by Jakob Peter Schechs (d.1659):

Oh God! hear my sighing and complaints,
Let me in my need not despair;
You know my pain, Know also my heart:
You have presented these burdens, help me
    also to bear them.
I know you have never forgotten me.
In the midst of need Think of God,
Who has already redeemed me through his
    suffering on the cross.

Each phrase of the melody is preceded by a chromatic introduction, the reiterating descending second illustrates the "sighs" of the text.

LOUIS-JAMES-ALFRED LEFÉBURE-WÉLY
VERSET IN F

For 30 years, in church and in recital, the "Auber of the Organ" reigned as "Prince of Organists"—the most prominent, the most universally recognized, and certainly the most popular Parisian organist of his day. Lefébure-Wély was renowned for his improvisations (praised by Saint-Saëns and considered by Alexandre Guilmant as the finest improviser France had produced). As a composer he was an enthusiastic purveyor of light, elegant, and successful music that combined a sparkling melodic verve with facile compositional techniques.

This Verset is from the collection *L'Organiste Moderne* published in 1867. It is dedicated to the pastor of Saint-Sulpice and, like all the pieces in the volume, is based on "a theme improvised upon during Masses at Saint-Sulpice between 1867 and 1869."

FRANZ LISZT
WEIMAR'S VOLKSLIED

"Weimar's Folksong" was composed around 1857 to words by Peter Cornelius, "Down from the peak of the Wartburg a breeze blows and turns to sound." Originally for male chorus and orchestra, Liszt arranged it for organ and also for piano. It is a theme with two variations and a recapitulation of the refrain.

FELIX MENDELSSOHN
ANDANTE WITH VARIATIONS

Mendelssohn composed his Six Organ Sonatas at the request of a London publisher acting on the initiative of some English organists who were familiar with his masterly performances on the organ in London and in Birmingham. In a letter of December 17, 1844, Mendelssohn wrote that he was soon to send a parcel of twelve organ pieces. This *Andante with Variations,* completed July 23, 1844, was a part of the parcel that remained unpublished until Novello issued it posthumously in 1898.

GIOVANNI PIERLUIGI DA PALESTRINA
RICERCARE

Giovanni Pierluigi was born in the little town of Palestrina in the Roman Campagna and represents, with Josquin des Près, Orlando di Lassus, and Tomás Luis de Victoria, the golden age of church music. Palestrina studied in Rome where he was a chorister at St. Maria Maggiore. He became organist of St. Agapito, Palestrina, in 1544 and after the Bishop of Palestrina was elected Pope Julius III, he was appointed *maestro di cappella* of the Cappella Giulia in Rome. He later served two of Rome's greatest churches as *maestro di cappella*, St. John Lateran (1555–60) and St. Maria Maggiore (1561–66).

A Ricercare (Italian "to seek out") is an instrumental musical composition that was popular during the 16th and 17th centuries in which one or more themes is developed through melodic *imitation*. Palestrina left only one manuscript volume containing 17 ricercari in two suites.

JOSEPH RHEINBERGER
VISION

Born in Vaduz, Liechtenstein, Rheinberger was organist at a church there by the age of seven. His family moved to Munich when he was twelve and he remained in that city the rest of his life. He was professor of piano and composition at the Munich Conservatory. His reputation as an organ teacher was unparalleled and students flocked to him from all over the world, including Horatio Parker, George Whitefield Chadwick, Frederick S. Converse, Sidney Homer, and Louis Adolphe Coerne from America. He published 199 opus numbers but today is chiefly remembered for the 20 organ sonatas. Nicolas Slonimsky has characterized his works as "remarkable for their dignity, formal perfection, and consummate technical mastery, if not for inventive power."

CAMILLE SAINT-SAËNS
IMPROVISATION, OP. 150, NO. 3

As a prodigy, Saint-Saëns was equaled only by Mozart. A brilliant, pianist, organist, and composer, he won first prize in organ at the Paris Conservatoire at the age of 16. He was organist of the Church of Saint-Merry (1853–58) and La Madeleine (1858–77), resigning to devote himself to concertizing and composing.

Sept Improvisations were composed between December 9, 1916 and February 12, 1917, and are dedicated to one of Saint-Saëns's former students at the École Niedermeyer, Eugène Gigout. At the time Gigout was professor of organ at the Paris Conservatoire. Saint-Saëns premiered Opus 150 in Marseille's Théâtre des Nations on March 25, 1917.

AMBROISE THOMAS
OFFERTOIRE IN C MAJOR

Best known as the composer of the opera *Mignon,* Thomas was a teacher at the Paris Conservatoire (one of his students was Massenet) and in 1871 succeeded Daniel Auber as director. The following year he approved César Franck's appointment as professor of organ. Between 1858 and 1860 he published several organ works, including this *Offertoire,* in the church music journal edited by Louis Niedermeyer, *La Matrîse.*

LOUIS VIERNE
ARABESQUE, OP. 31, NO. 15

An organ student at the Paris Conservatoire of César Franck and Charles-Marie Widor, Vierne was appointed organist of Notre Dame Cathedral in 1900. In addition to six monumental symphonies for the organ he wrote two sets of 24 pieces: those in *style libre,* or on free themes, and a set of Fantasy Pieces. The first set, published in 1914 and dedicated to his students and friends, was on two staves and intended for the organ, manuals only, or the harmonium.

In the exposition and final restatement of the hauntingly modal *Arabesque,* measures in G major alternate with those based on the whole-tone scale.

JOHN WARD
AYRE

Born in Canterbury, John Ward is remembered for his madrigals, anthems, and virginal music. This *Ayre* was originally for two bass viols and organ.

CHARLES-MARIE WIDOR
MÉDITATION FROM *SYMPHONIE I,* OP. 13

Within two years of succeeding Lefébure-Wély in 1870 as organist of Saint-Sulpice, where he presided over the largest organ in France, Charles-Marie Widor published his first four organ symphonies. Consisting of five to seven movements, they exploit the symphonic instruments of the French organ builder Aristide Cavaillé-Coll to the ultimate degree. This *Méditation,* the sixth movement of the first symphony, is the only movement Widor never changed in the many subsequent printings.

ROLLIN SMITH

Ricercare

GIOVANNI PIERLUIGI DA PALESTRINA
1525–1594

* Variante

Ayre

I. Quintadena 8' or Bourdon 8' and Nazard 2⅔'
II. Bourdon and Gemshorn 8'

JOHN WARD
1571–c.1638

Chacone in F Major

LOUIS COUPERIN
1626–1661

à Monsieur Detrische
Conseiller et Reçepueur Génréral de sa Maiesté Catholicque en Doesflandre, &c.

Voix Humaine
in the 1st tone, Op. 2

I. Jeu doux: Bourdon, &c.
II. Voix humaine, 8' Bourdon, tremblant

LAMBERT CHAUMONT
c.1635–1712

à Monsieur Detrische
Conseiller et Reçepueur Génréral de sa Maiesté Catholicque en Doesflandre, &c.

Trio par Contrefugue

in the 6th tone, Op. 1

Jeu éclattant: Bourdon, Montre, Nazard, Tierce, &c.

LAMBERT CHAUMONT
c.1635–1712

Pastorale
BWV 590

JOHANN SEBASTIAN BACH
1685–1750

Offertoire for Easter on
O Filii et Filiæ

Grand-Orgue   8' Montre, Bourdon, 4' Prestant, 2⅔' Nasard,
        2' Quarte de Nasard, and 8' Trompette

Positif 8' Bourdon, 4' Prestant

[Récit] Cornet (8' 4' 2⅔' 2' 1⅗')

JEAN-FRANÇOIS DANDRIEU
1681/2–1738

Prelude and Fugue

in D major

GEORGE FRIDERIC HANDEL
1685–1759

Prelude

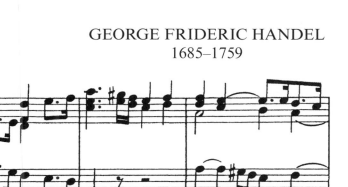

Fugue

Concerto No. 13

The Cuckoo and the Nightingale

I. Orchestra
II. Organ

GEORGE FRIDERIC HANDEL
1685–1759

43

49

Offertoire

in C Major

AMBROISE THOMAS
1811–1896

Supprimez les jeux d'anches.

Diminuendo - - - - - - - - - - - - - -

Andantino

FRANZ JOSEPH HAYDN
1732–1809

O God! Hear My Sighs

Ach Gott! erhör mein Seufzen

JOHANN LUDWIG KREBS
1713–1780

Andante with Variations

FELIX MENDELSSOHN
1809–1847

a Tempo

[poco rit.]

[Tempo I]

à Mr. l'Abbé Hamon, Curé de St-Sulpice

Verset

in F Major

RÉCIT   Hautbois
POSITIF   Flûtes de 4 et 2
Gd.-ORGUE Viole de gambe   LOUIS-A.-J. LEFÉBURE-WÉLY
PÉDALE   Bourdon 16   1817–1869

Offertorium

CHARLES GOUNOD
1818–1893

+32'

Communion

Jeux doux 8 et 16 pieds.

CHARLES GOUNOD
1818–1893

Weimar's Volkslied

FRANZ LISZT
1811-1886

O World, I E'en Must Leave Thee

O Welt, ich muß dich lassen

Op. 122, No. 11

JOHANNES BRAHMS
1833–1897

Andantino
in G Minor

Swell: 8' Viole d'amour, 4' Flûte octaviante, 8' Hautbois
Great: 8' Bourdon, 8' Gambe, 4' Flûte d'amour
Choir: 8' Bourdon, 4' Flûte
Pedal: 16' and 8' Flûtes

CÉSAR FRANCK
1822-1890

Offertoire
in G Minor

Swell: 8' Viole d'amour, 4' Flûte octaviante, 8' Hautbois
Great: 8' Bourdon, 8' Gambe, 4' Flûte d'amour
Choir: 8' Bourdon, 4' Flûte
Pedal: 16' and 8' Flûtes

CÉSAR FRANCK
1822-1890

à Eugène Gigout

Improvisation

Op. 150, No. 3

Récit: Voix humaine, [Bourdon 8 et Trémolo]
Positif: Flûtes 8 et 4
Pédale: Bourdons 16 et 8

CAMILLE SAINT-SAËNS
1835–1921

à Monsieur A. Cavaillé-Coll

Méditation

from *Symphonie No. 1,* Op. 13, No. 1

G Flûte 8
R Gambes 8
Péd. Basses 8 et 16

CHARLES-MARIE WIDOR
1844–1937

Visione

from *Twelve Characteristic Pieces,* Op. 156

JOSEPH RHEINBERGER
1839–1901

to Charles Heinroth

Cantilène
in G Major, Op. 71, No. 1

I. Flute and Salicional
II. Dulciana and Flute

ARTHUR FOOTE
1853–1937

Andantino espressivo

à mon Émile Bourdon

Arabesque

Op. 31, No. 15

G. Flûte harmonique
R. Gambe
Péd. Bourdons 8' 16'. Claviers accouplés.

LOUIS VIERNE
1870–1937

G. Fonds doux 8

[-Gt. to Ped.]

G.R. *mf*

Péd. G.R.

R. *p*

Péd. **R.**

Rall. poco a poco

Choral

Op. 37, No. 4

RÉCIT	Fonds 4, 8, 16, Anches préparées
POSITIF	Fonds 8
Gd.-ORGUE	Fonds 4, 8, 16
PÉDALE	Soubasse 16, Flûte 8
	Claviers accouplées

JOSEPH JONGEN
1873–1953

ajoutez progressivement les Anches et Mixtures du G^dO. Pos. et Ped.
add progressively Reeds and Mixture, to Great, Choir and Ped.

Janvier 1911.

Improvisation
on the English Chorale
"Nearer, My God, to Thee"
Op. 81

SIGFRID KARG-ELERT
1877–1933

Original Melody

„Nä - her, mein Gott, zu dir, nä - her zu dir!" Das soll die Lo - sung sein, das mein Pa - nier!
Nä - her, mein Gott, zu dir, hö - re mein Fleh'n: läßt du die Trüb-sals-flut hoch um mich gehn,
„Nä - her, mein Gott, zu dir, nä - her zu dir!" soll jetzt die Lo - sung sein, jetzt mein Pa - nier!

Wie du auch füh-rest hier, nä - her nur, Gott, zu dir, nä - her, mein Gott, zu dir, nä - her zu dir!
hilf auch durch Trüb-sal mir, nä - her mein Gott, zu dir, nä - her, mein Gott, zu dir! Hö - re mein Fleh'n!
Jetzt schei - de ich von hier, nimm mich hin - auf zu dir, nimm mich hin - auf zu dir, Va - ter, zu dir!

123

* Or this Episode may be played an 8ve lower without 16 feet stops.

Epilog (Ad astra).